Cynthia Levinson   Illustrated by Mirelle Ortega

FREE TO LEARN

How Alfredo Lopez Fought for the Right to Go to School

Å atheneum **ATHENEUM BOOKS FOR YOUNG READERS** • NEW YORK LONDON TORONTO SYDNEY NEW DELHI

Alfredo had so many questions the day before second grade started! He popped up and down in front of his mother.

"How will I find the right room?" he asked. "Is Jaime in my class? Will my teacher speak Spanish so I can understand her this year?"

But Amá just looked away and didn't answer. He knew what that meant—no more questions! Oh well, he'd find out tomorrow.

The next morning, though, Alfredo did not find first-day-of-school migas for breakfast, fresh laces for his sneakers, or a sharp number two pencil. Did that mean there was no school after all?

But a few minutes later, he watched as Jaime and other children streamed past his house. Confused, Alfredo peppered Amá with more questions.

"Why does Jaime get to go to school? Why can't I? What makes me different?"

Amá clamped her mouth shut. Alfredo stomped outside and kicked up clods of dirt.

"I'll miss story time," he grumbled, "and art and recess."

"Uh-oh. How will I learn English?"

Alfredo was born in an adobe hut in the town of Jalpa in the state of Zacatecas, Mexico. He had one toy—a tiny plastic car—to call his own.

He played by the light of a smelly kerosene lantern until bedtime, when he slept on a thin mat on the ground. Because Amá and Apá couldn't find jobs, the family sometimes went hungry.

Apá's brother, Alfredo's tío, lived in the town of Tyler in the state of Texas, USA.

"There are jobs here," he wrote.

Desperate for work, Amá and Apá had no choice but to leave Alfredo with his grandparents and join Tío in Texas.

By the time Alfredo was seven, he had to work too. Every sunup he led Abuelo's cows to pasture, then fetched them back at sundown.

He hoed, planted, weeded, picked,

and hauled corn and beans.

Worn out, he slumped on the hard wooden bench at school.

"When will Amá and Apá come back?" he asked Abuela. "What's it like in the US? Can I go too?" But she didn't answer because she didn't know.

On New Year's Eve two years later, Alfredo's tío arrived with happy news. "It's time to go to the US!"

"Can we leave right now?" Alfredo asked. "How long will it take? When will we get there?"

He squeezed his grandparents goodbye, then rode a jouncy bus with Tío, gazing into darkness hour after hour. Asleep and bundled in blankets, he slipped into Texas in a pickup, unseen by Border Patrol.

Alfredo awoke in a New Year to a world of wonders. Amá! Apá! Plus baby José, born right here. So many hugs! And a home with a bathroom, a refrigerator, soft beds.

In his new classroom, Alfredo found a desk, books, and crayons to call his own. At lunch, a boy named Jaime handed him a carton of milk.

So this was the US!

But the next summer, a new state law decreed:

If you were not born here
If you are not a citizen
If you do not have proper documents,
you are illegal.

So,
You cannot go to school.

Alfredo didn't know he was considered illegal. He only knew that when the school year started, he wasn't welcome.

This was the US too.

After Alfredo recited his bedtime prayers, Amá whispered to Apá, "If Alfredo can't go to school, there's no reason to stay."

"Should we leave our jobs, our home, go back to Mexico?" Apá asked.

"No. José is a citizen. He belongs here."

"We all belong here."

"Then we have to fight the law," she said.

"Yes," he agreed. "But if anyone finds out we don't have papers, we'll be deported. We must not tell Alfredo."

Every morning, Alfredo waved at Jaime walking to school, then waved again in the afternoon. He wondered who Jaime had sat with at lunch and story time, who he'd played with at recess. Meanwhile, he rolled a ball to José and helped Amá with chores.

After Alfredo spent a whole week at home, Amá woke him before sunup.

"Am I going to school?" he asked. She looked away.

Alfredo squeezed into the car, packed with clothes, food, and the television set. "In case we have to go to Mexico," Apá said.

"Why would we go back?" Alfredo asked. No one answered.

They bumped over Tyler's brick streets to the federal courthouse.

Hushed, Alfredo and his parents avoided the main entrance and slipped through a back door. Alfredo saw jail cells straight ahead. No one spoke as the family rode the prisoners' elevator up to the courtroom.

Alfredo wanted to ask, "Are they sending us to jail? To Mexico? Why are we here?" But his voice felt stuck in his throat.

"Hear ye! All rise," called a clerk. Everyone jumped up. "The Honorable William Wayne Justice presiding." A stern man in a long black robe asked Amá and Apá to describe their jobs.

"Slicing thorns off roses is hard work," Amá said, "but it's better than having no work in Mexico."

Apá said he came home from the iron factory coated with grime. "It's worth it to feed the children and send Alfredo to school."

A lawyer named Peter then stood to argue their case. Alfredo didn't follow what Peter said, but he heard Amá murmur a prayer.

"The Tyler schools," Peter began, "admit undocumented children from every country except Mexico. That's not fair!"

He pointed to Alfredo's two-year-old brother. "José will be able to go to school here. Why can't Alfredo? They live in the same house! The only difference is they were born on opposite sides of the border."

Peter concluded by quoting the Fourteenth Amendment to the US Constitution. "'No state shall . . . deny to any person within its jurisdiction the equal protection of the laws.' This means everyone must be treated the same way. But the law that keeps children born in Mexico out of school treats them differently from others. So Texas's law is not just unfair. It's unconstitutional!"

The school district's lawyer, John, disagreed. "The Fourteenth Amendment applies only to people who are in America legally. Alfredo is here illegally. He doesn't deserve to be treated like everyone else."

Peter responded, "The Constitution says every person in America has the same rights. Tyler must teach all children—including Alfredo—no matter where they're from or how they got here."

On the way home, Alfredo exclaimed, "We're not going to Mexico!" Amá and Apá smiled. Still, he wondered if he'd have to keep doing chores forever.

But he didn't have to wait and do chores forever. Two days after the hearing, Alfredo's parents told him he could go back to school! Judge Justice had declared Texas's law unconstitutional. He'd ordered Tyler to admit all undocumented students, because every child should be "given a chance."

The next morning, Alfredo found new shoelaces and a sharp number two pencil beside his migas. Then, he and Jaime walked to T. J. Austin Elementary.

"Which is my desk?" he asked his teacher. "What page are we on? Are there crayons? When's recess? What's for lunch?"

Alfredo knew what made him different from the other kids—he hadn't been born in the United States. But he had learned that didn't matter. He had the same right to go to school as Jaime—and everyone else.

Because the US Constitution says so.

DOE, BOE, LOE, AND ROE

This book is a work of historical fiction—a made-up story based on actual events. All the people are real, although they didn't necessarily say or do exactly what I wrote. For instance, Alfredo didn't ask where his classroom was, and Peter sounded more like a lawyer in the courtroom.

Here's what really happened.

In 1975, the Texas legislature passed a law that prohibited the use of public money to educate undocumented students. In 1977, the Tyler Independent School District (TISD) started charging these students a thousand dollars per year. Since most of them couldn't afford to pay, they could no longer attend school.

Mike McAndrew, a social worker at Immaculate Conception Catholic Church, arranged with two local lawyers, Roberta Rodkin and Larry Daves, and with Peter Roos, a lawyer with the Mexican American Legal Defense and Educational Fund (MALDEF), to sue James Plyler, the superintendent of TISD. They talked with a dozen families, but only four agreed to sue. Most were, understandably, too scared of being deported if immigration agents identified them in court.

To protect the families' identities, the lawyers assigned aliases.

- Felix Hernandez became Boe.
- Rosario and José Robles became Doe.
- Humberto and Jackeline Alvarez became Loe.
- Lidia and José Lopez became Roe. In court papers, Alfredo is referred to as "A. Roe."

Judge William Wayne Justice heard the case (which was initially called *Doe v. Plyler* and later changed to *Plyler v. Doe*) in his courtroom in Tyler, Texas, on September 9, 1977. Alfredo and the other families courageously attended the hearing, which the judge scheduled for six a.m., when no one else was around. Two days later, Judge Justice ordered TISD to admit undocumented students for free.

His decision, though, applied only to the Tyler Independent School District. Other districts in Texas continued to enforce the state's law. For three years, an unknown number of undocumented students were either barred from school altogether or attended secret schools in church basements and elsewhere. Meanwhile, the Tyler school district appealed the ruling to a higher court, hoping to have the judge's decision rejected—but their strategy backfired. The US Court of Appeals for the Fifth Circuit agreed with Judge Justice and stated that his ruling should apply across Texas.

The State of Texas and TISD appealed again—this time to the US Supreme Court, where the vote was close. Four of the nine justices believed that state legislatures—not federal courts—should decide whether schools had to admit undocumented students. However, a majority of five justices declared that Texas's law was unconstitutional. Their opinion, announced on June 15, 1982, stated that children "should not be left on the streets uneducated," no matter where they were born. Alfredo, then fourteen, told a reporter that day that he would feel "terrible" if he couldn't go to school.

At every stage of the court fight, the families' lawyers based their argument on the Fourteenth Amendment. Every person deserves "equal protection of the laws."

ALFREDO, LIDIA, AND JOSÉ LOPEZ

Alfredo was nine years old when he entered the US in January 1977. Because he didn't speak English, the Tyler Independent School District placed him in second grade and then had him repeat the year beginning in the fall. He and his three younger siblings didn't learn for seventeen years why Alfredo missed school for a week, why they spent a day in court, or that their parents had risked deportation. Amá and Apá were good at keeping secrets! Lidia and José Lopez are also modest. They never boasted about their role in ensuring that millions of undocumented students across America could go to school.

In 2007, on the twenty-fifth anniversary of the Supreme Court's decision, MALDEF honored Lidia and José with a ceremony in San Antonio, Texas, which their children and grandchildren proudly attended.

JUDGE WILLIAM WAYNE JUSTICE

Born in Athens, Texas, in 1920, William Wayne Justice started helping out at his father's law office when he was seven years old. So his father, Will, changed the name on the door to "W. D. Justice and Son." The following year, a neighbor told eight-year-old Wayne not to play with a Black child. That was the first time he became aware of racism, and he never forgot it.

Justice became a successful lawyer, and in 1968, President Lyndon Johnson appointed him to be one of two federal district court judges in Tyler. Over the next thirty years, Judge Justice ordered public schools to desegregate, penitentiaries to stop treating prisoners inhumanely, colleges to admit male students with long hair, and homes for disabled people to provide mental health support and other services.

Many residents of Tyler disliked his decisions and plastered stickers on their car bumpers calling him the "most hated man in Texas." Others, however, praised his decisions and said, "You got Justice, or no justice."

As for the *Plyler* case, a Texan wrote him, "Your decision is a bum one." Nevertheless, Judge Justice stated, "That's the case I'm most proud of." Years later even former superintendent James Plyler admitted that the judge had made the right decision. "Those youngsters needed an education," he said. "I'm glad we could receive them in the school district."

AUTHOR'S NOTE

Above all, I am deeply grateful to Alfredo, Angie, Lidia, and José Lopez for allowing me to share—and fictionalize—their story. Along with Kassie Lopez, Faviola (Lopez) Tizcareño, Peter Roos, John Hardy, Roberta Rodkin Thami, Larry Daves, Michael McAndrew, Monsignor Milam Joseph, Ruth Epstein, Virginia Raymond, and others, they spent many hours explaining the historical events to me. Sleuthing for the families' testimony, which was redacted and hidden by court order, became a saga; I am indebted to Jessica Landry for sharing their statements.

This case has touched my life in multiple ways. In 1980, while the case was working its way through the court system, my family and I moved to Texas, where my husband has taught at the University of Texas School of Law. Librarians there provided me with invaluable source material. Just two years after the Supreme Court's decision, I began working at the Texas Education Agency (TEA), which had joined the lawsuit against the four families—but then, following another case decided by Judge Justice, TEA helped schools provide bilingual education to children.

I am not alone, though, in being touched by this case. All Americans, whether or not they are documented, benefit from children getting a free public education.

SOURCE NOTES

"given a chance": Doe v. Plyler, 458 F. Supp. 569, US District Court for the Eastern District of Texas (1978).

"should not be left on the streets uneducated": Plyler v. Doe, 457 U.S. 202 (1982).

"terrible": Alfredo Lopez interview, NBC News, June 15, 1982.

"most hated man in Texas": Denise Gamino, "A Giant of Texas History," Austin American-Statesman, October 15, 2009.

"You got Justice, or no justice": Jill Lepore, "Is Education a Fundamental Right?," New Yorker, September 3, 2018.

"Your decision is a bum one": Memo from V. J. Neugebauer, September 20, 1978, https://tarltonapps.law.utexas.edu /exhibits/ww_justice/documents_2/Plyler_letter_1_1978. pdf.

"That's the case I'm most proud of": Hiroshi Motomura, Immigration Outside the Law (Oxford University Press, 2014), 9.

"Those youngsters . . . school district": Catherine Winter, "A Supreme Court Case 35 Years Ago Yields a Supply of Emboldened DACA Students Today," APM Reports, August 21, 2017, https://www.apmreports.org.

SELECTED BIBLIOGRAPHY

Articles

Belejack, Barbara. "The Texas Cases That Opened the Schoolhouse Door to Undocumented Immigrant Children." Texas Observer, July 13, 2007.

Lepore, Jill. "Is Education a Fundamental Right?" New Yorker, September 3, 2018.

Mendoza, Alexander. "The Building of an East Texas Barrio: A Brief Overview of the Creation of a Mexican American Community in Northeast Tyler." East Texas Historical Journal 47, no. 2 (article 9): 26–37.

Olivas, Michael A. "The Story of Plyler v. Doe: The Education of Undocumented Children and the Polity." Monograph, University of Houston Law Center, 2004. https://www .law.uh.edu/ihelg/monograph/05-09.pdf.

Raymond, Virginia Marie. "Mexican Americans Write Toward Justice in Texas, 1973–1982." PhD diss., University of Texas at Austin, 2007. https://repositories.lib.utexas .edu/handle/2152/6260.

Richardson, Laura, and Jo Clifton. "William Wayne Justice: An Interview." Texas Observer, January 20, 1978, 3–8.

Williams, Jamie. "Children Versus Texas: The Legacy of Plyler v. Doe." University of California Berkeley School of Law, paper for Professor Stephen Sugarman, April 27, 2011, https://www.law.berkeley.edu/files/Children_v._Texas _Williams.pdf.

Books

Driver, Justin. The Schoolhouse Gate: Public Education, the Supreme Court, and the Battle for the American Mind. New York: Pantheon, 2018.

Minian, Ana Raquel. Undocumented Lives: The Untold Story of Mexican Migration. Cambridge: Harvard University Press, 2018.

Court Filings

All legal and amicus briefs, arguments, and testimony (redacted), and all related opinions for the Eastern District of Texas, the US Court of Appeals for the Fifth Circuit, and the US Supreme Court.

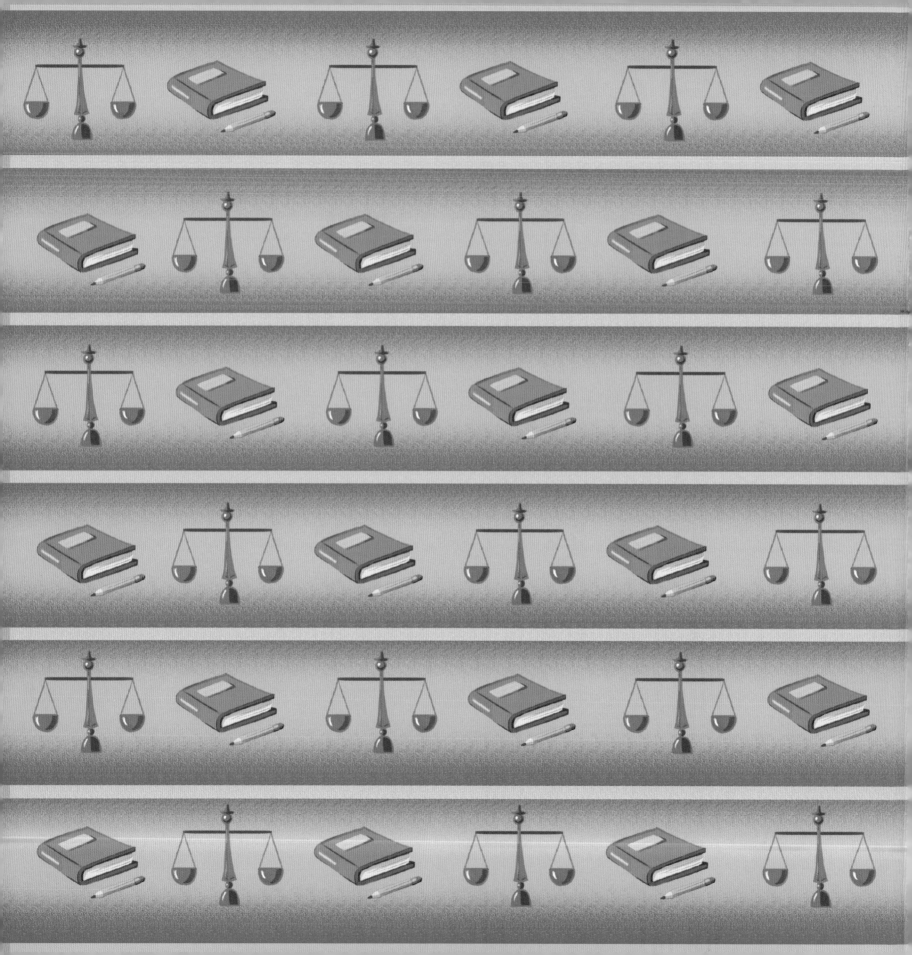